AF228476

Arabian Horses

by Grace Hansen

Abdo Kids Jumbo is an Imprint of Abdo Kids
abdobooks.com

abdobooks.com

Published by Abdo Kids, a division of ABDO, P.O. Box 398166, Minneapolis, Minnesota 55439.
Copyright © 2020 by Abdo Consulting Group, Inc. International copyrights reserved in all countries.
No part of this book may be reproduced in any form without written permission from the publisher.
Abdo Kids Jumbo™ is a trademark and logo of Abdo Kids.

Printed in the United States of America, North Mankato, Minnesota.

052019

092019

Photo Credits: Depositphotos Enterprise, iStock, Shutterstock

Production Contributors: Teddy Borth, Jennie Forsberg, Grace Hansen
Design Contributors: Dorothy Toth, Pakou Moua

Library of Congress Control Number: 2018963349

Publisher's Cataloging-in-Publication Data

Names: Hansen, Grace, author.

Title: Arabian horses / by Grace Hansen.

Description: Minneapolis, Minnesota : Abdo Kids, 2020 | Series: Horses set 2 |
    Includes online resources and index.

Identifiers: ISBN 9781532185632 (lib. bdg.) | ISBN 9781532186615 (ebook) |
    ISBN 9781532187100 (Read-to-me ebook)

Subjects: LCSH: Arabian horse--Juvenile literature. | Horses--Juvenile
    literature.

Classification: DDC 636.112--dc23

Table of Contents

Arabian Horses

Arabian horses are one of the oldest and most **recognized** horse breeds in the world.

This breed first appeared more than 2,000 years ago on the **Arabian Peninsula**. They were bred to be smart, good-natured, and easy to train. Today, Arabian owners enjoy very good horses.

Arabian horses have wedge-shaped heads. They have large eyes and wide foreheads. Some have a small **bulge** between their eyes.

8

Their ears and **muzzles**

are small. Their **nostrils**

are large.

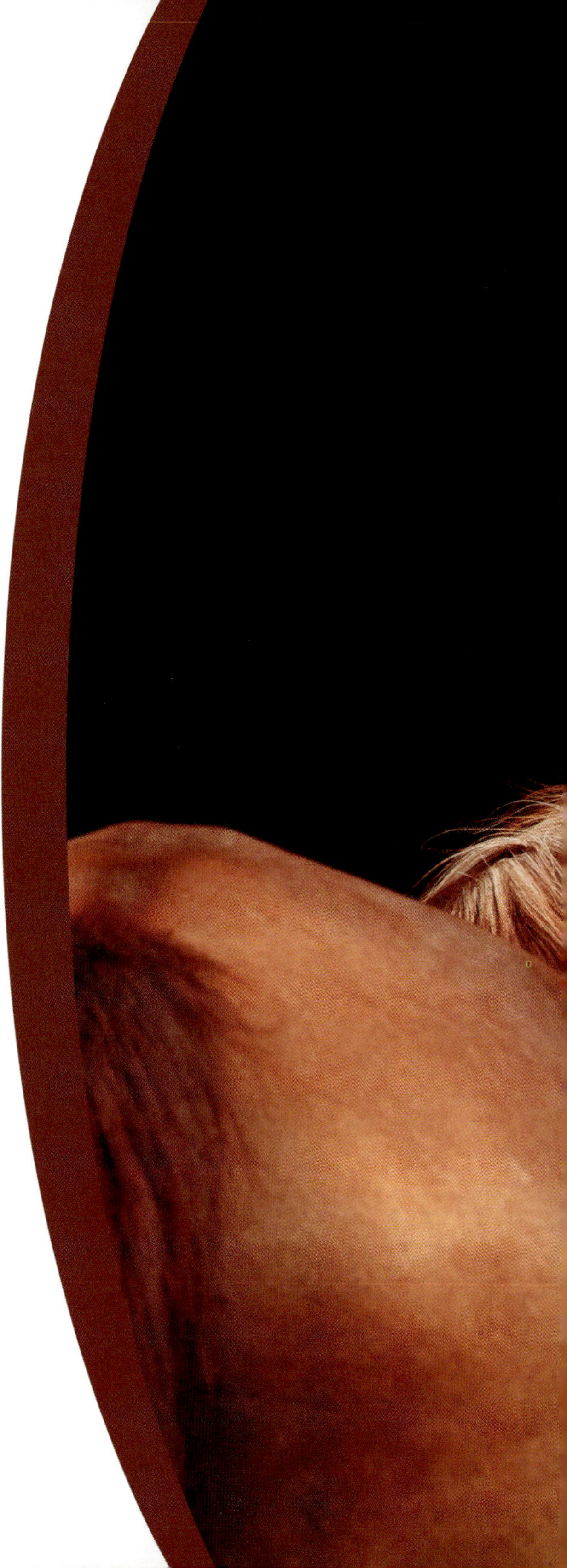

Arabians have short backs.

Their tails sit high on their

strong **rumps**.

Some Arabian horses have

longer, leaner muscles. Horses

that are leaner are great for

long rides and racing.

4
9

Arabian horses should be 14.1 to 15.1 **hands** tall. They usually weigh between 800 and 1,000 pounds (363 to 454 kg).

Arabian horses come in five
main colors. These are **bay**,
gray, chestnut, black, and **roan**.

Personality

Arabians are known for their good personalities. However, they are **hot-blooded** horses. This makes them sensitive and smart. Owners must handle them with patience and respect.

21

More Facts

- Arabian horses are one of the oldest and purest horse breeds.

- Arabian horses are very good with people. They are loving and good natured.

- These horses are unique from other breeds in many ways. One way is that they have fewer rib, lumbar, and vertebra bones.

Glossary

Arabian Peninsula – a piece of land in southwestern Asia that sits between the Red Sea and the Persian Gulf.

bay – brown body color with black legs, mane, tail, and ears.

bulge – a lump or bump.

hand – a unit of measurement of a horse's height, equal to 4 inches (10.16 cm).

hot-blooded – being a Thoroughbred or having Arab blood.

muzzle – the part of the head of some animals that contains the nose, jaws, and mouth.

nostrils – the two openings on the nose.

roan – a color made up by an even mixture of colored and white hair.

rump – the hind part of the body of a mammal.

Index

Abdo Kids ONLINE

FREE! ONLINE MULTIMEDIA RESOURCES

Visit **abdokids.com** to access crafts, games, videos, and more!